"The moment I started reading this book, the hair went up on my neck. I blasted through it in a night, thrilled by the energy. Shields doesn't wear out the form; it keeps doing remarkable tricks on the reader's brain right to the finish. Stunning."

Jonathan Lethem

"A sort of existential mixtape, and at the heart of it all is how others see us, what they imagine of us. 'Do you think anyone can understand anyone else, and if not, what are any of us doing other than walking around trapped for an eternity in our own space suits?' *The Very Last Interview* attempts to answer this question and at the same time complicates it in an utterly thrilling way. I love this book."

Nick Flynn

"David Shields, the wild card in contemporary non-fiction, always challenges the presumptions of genre. His terrific new book, *The Very Last Interview*, is alternately hilarious, sad, and, for any author, excruciatingly recognizable. By submitting to a self-inquisition, Shields demonstrates how much of our self-image is determined or undermined by the outside world, how much the voice of that doppelgänger feeds our doubt and inevitable sense of failure. Ironically, the book itself is a triumph of honesty and craft."

"Not for the first time when confronted with a book by David Shields, I approached with skepticism, was initially irritated, then charmed, and ended up being thoroughly captivated."

Geoff Dyer

"Engaging, lively, funny, and fascinating, partly for the way the questions answer themselves and partly for the gaps we have to imagine when the questions are answered in a way that we can't hear. Shields's preoccupations are very much in evidence, but I saw a lot of myself in it, as will, I would think, most readers. Quite wonderful."

Charles Baxter

The Very Last Interview

THE TROUBLE WITH MEN *Reflections on Sex, Love, Marriage, Porn, and Power*

NOBODY HATES TRUMP MORE THAN TRUMP *An Intervention*

OTHER PEOPLE *Takes & Mistakes*

WAR IS BEAUTIFUL *The* New York Times *Pictorial Guide to the Glamour of Armed Conflict*

THAT THING YOU DO WITH YOUR MOUTH *The Sexual Autobiography of Samantha Matthews, as told to David Shields*

LIFE IS SHORT—ART IS SHORTER *In Praise of Brevity*
co-editor with Elizabeth Cooperman

I THINK YOU'RE TOTALLY WRONG *A Quarrel*
co-author with Caleb Powell

SALINGER
co-author with Shane Salerno

HOW LITERATURE SAVED MY LIFE

FAKES *An Anthology of Pseudo-Interviews, Faux-Lectures, Quasi-Letters, "Found" Texts, and Other Fraudulent Artifacts*
co-editor with Matthew Vollmer

JEFF, ONE LONELY GUY
co-author with Jeff Ragsdale and Michael Logan

THE INEVITABLE *Contemporary Writers Confront Death*
co-editor with Bradford Morrow

REALITY HUNGER *A Manifesto*

THE THING ABOUT LIFE IS THAT ONE DAY YOU'LL BE DEAD

BODY POLITIC *The Great American Sports Machine*

ENOUGH ABOUT YOU *Notes Toward the New Autobiography*

BASEBALL IS JUST BASEBALL *The Understated Ichiro*

BLACK PLANET *Facing Race During an NBA Season*

REMOTE *Reflections on Life in the Shadow of Celebrity*

HANDBOOK FOR DROWNING *A Novel in Stories*

DEAD LANGUAGES *A Novel*

HEROES *A Novel*

The Very Last
Interview

DAVID SHIELDS

nyrb   **New York Review Books** New York

This is a New York Review Book

published by The New York Review of Books

435 Hudson Street, New York, NY 10014

www.nyrb.com

The author wishes to express his deep gratitude to the University of Washington for the Loren Douglas Milliman Distinguished Writer-in-Residence position, which enabled him to finish this book.

LIBRARY OF CONGRESS CATALOGING-IN-PUBLICATION DATA
Names: Shields, David, 1956– author.
Title: The very last interview / by David Shields.
Description: New York : New York Review Books, [2022]
Identifiers: LCCN 2021027766 (print) | LCCN 2021027767 (ebook)
    | ISBN 9781681376424 (paperback) | ISBN 9781681376431
    (ebook)
Subjects: LCSH: Shields, David, 1956– —Miscellanea.
Classification: LCC PS3569.H4834 Z46 2022 (print) | LCC
    PS3569.H4834 (ebook) | DDC 813/.54 [B]—dc23
LC record available at https://lccn.loc.gov/2021027766
LC ebook record available at https://lccn.loc.gov/2021027767

ISBN 978-1-68137-642-4
Available as an electronic book; ISBN 978-1-68137-643-1

Printed in the United States of America on acid-free paper.

10 9 8 7 6 5 4 3 2 1

Contents

Beneath every question is an elegy.

—ADAM CLAY

Remarks are not literature.

—GERTRUDE STEIN

Process

Life isn't about saying the right thing. And it's certainly not about tape-recording everything so that you have to endure it more than once. Life is about failing. It is about letting the tape play.

—Jonathan Goldstein

You ready?

Ready to roll?

Is this thing on?

Can you sit up a little in your chair and turn toward me?

We're six feet apart, wouldn't you say?

Any chance you can project your voice out a little louder?

Are you hearing as much feedback as I am?

Do you have to be anywhere else later this morning, by which I mean do you have a "hard out" of, say, noon?

I have no particular agenda going in, do you?

Might we just start and see where our conversation takes us?

How—more broadly—do you choose the subjects for your books?

What was the origin of your most recent book?

How did it develop, then?

Why would you choose that as your material?

Doesn't it seem somewhat counterproductive to pursue that particular subject in this day and age?

This latest book is, in my view, sui generis. The form is indistinguishable from the book's "content." Which came first—the approach or the argument?

How many times have you been sued?

"The law is my muse"—what does that mean?

Do you really believe that?

How can you tell a good idea for a book from a bad idea for a book?

When you get a good idea for a book, what do you do next?

Where do these ideas—good, bad, indifferent—come from?

Have you ever had a great idea for a book and then discarded it?

If you're working on a new book now, might you wind up discarding it?

If you discard it, can I have it?

While you're writing a book, do you discuss it with fellow practitioners?

Is there really such a thing as a writing "community"?

Do you ever wish you could tell a story in a more straightforward manner?

Do you miss being a novelist?

This is a wildly overused trope, but some of the reviews of your earlier books said you had the potential to become something approximating your generation's version of Salinger. You're now more like the baby boomers' Hermann Broch; doesn't that feel like quite a letdown?

Several of your books are very similar in approach; do you work on more than one at a time?

Do any of them feel to you redundant?

You once said to me—as a joke, I suppose—that all your books are "brief, collaborative, and plagiarized," but, really, what is the secret to your somewhat monomaniacal rate of production, especially the last decade?

"Perish into the work," I suppose, per the Kunitz dictum?

Did you always want to become a writer?

Why?

Which was the bigger influence—both of your parents being journalists or your childhood stutter?

What's the first thing you ever published, outside of college magazines?

Outside of academic journals?

Outside of magazines edited by your friends?

How do you find an agent?

Is it difficult?

How many agents have you had?

Is that a lot?

Seven agents but only one wife? Interesting.

Ex-wife? I see.

Recently? Sorry to hear that.

Did you encounter much rejection at first?

Do you still?

What have you learned from rejection?

According to E. M. Cioran, "Only one thing matters: learning to be the loser." Agree or disagree?

Another way to ask this is, are all writers "bottoms"?

Having read nearly all of your work, I'd say you're more than "half in love with easeful death." Any pushback on your part?

Are there any how-to books you would recommend?

Any you would counsel against?

What does John Casey mean when he says, "A writer needs only two things—an absolute commitment to tell the truth and low vaudeville cunning"?

Did you study with him at Iowa?

He stutters pretty badly, doesn't he?

Has he ever written directly about that, to your knowledge?

Does the title of his novel *The Half-Life of Happiness* mimic stuttering, in your view?

Do you keep a journal?

What's the worst book you've written?

Worst supposedly "great book" you've read?

Most influential, in a good way?

Is it true that you once drove from Providence to Berkeley to ask Leonard Michaels to release you from the stranglehold of his voice?

In a bad sense?

Do you write every day?

Do you have a "schedule"?

Does it ever seem odd to you that John Clayton, who was born and raised in Pittsburgh, pronounces "schedule" in the British manner?

So you're at it more or less all the time?

If you write a book and it's published and no one pays any attention, do you regret the trees felled in the forest?

Do you fervently wish for a MacArthur fellowship as validation of your existence?

Maybe apply next year?

How long did it take you to write your second novel?

Why so long?

Were you ever concerned that the material would go dead or "flat" on you?

Does this feeling ever wash over you: "When am I ever going to finish this, and will anyone find this of interest?"

What's more challenging—the research, the writing, or the rewriting?

Do you ever hire research assistants?

What do you pay?

May I email you my CV?

I've heard you're a big winnower; any tips in that realm?

How can you tell what to retain and what to jettison?

Are you good at absorbing criticism?

Do you mind, then, if I offer you a little constructive criticism about your last three books?

What makes you want to write another book?

To be blunt, why bother, when not that many people read each new book of yours anymore, do they?

For instance, has any book of yours sold even fifty thousand copies in hardcover? That would be every person in Pascagoula, Mississippi, but absolutely no one else.

Isn't there a sort of grace in knowing when to exit the stage?

Not being the bald, old dude drinking PBR at the punk show—if and when we have such shows again?

Are you, in effect, a dead man walking?

Are you a good titler, do you think?

Personally, I sort of like your titles, but why do they always remind me of lyrics from an emo band's first album?

Someone else already said that? LOL. Maybe I read it somewhere.

Do you have any writing rituals—lighting incense or plinking on the piano or reading poetry beforehand or whatever?

I still don't get it; can you explain again why you don't write fiction anymore?

Do you prefer the term "montage" or "assemblage" or "bricolage"?

Oh, I see—"collage"?

Might we not be able to map your devotion to "collage" —its polyphonic Cubism—onto your lifelong battle with stuttering?

Do you think of yourself now as more of a sculptor?

A conceptual artist?

A film editor?

I meant this figuratively, but now you're actively trying to make real movies?

Where do you get the money?

Are you secretly rich?

Ever worry about spreading yourself too thin?

Why does Helen Deutsch—a specialist in Samuel Johnson—call you an "amateur" in the eighteenth-century sense of the word?

Amo, amas, amat?

Do you take this as praise or put-down?

Taking it from the opposite angle: abstract expressionism permeates your work and has for decades. Whence your genuflection to Jackson Pollock?

Not your idol anymore?

It was exceedingly important, though, for you to correct Caleb's pronunciation?

Your father collected quotes; so do you, obviously. A couple of "wisdom" junkies?

"Magpies," perhaps—is that the better word?

When you put these scattered fragments together, how do you really know they will all come together?

I guess I'm asking, is there a method to your seeming madness?

A deeper structure, an ur-narrative?

How many of your books would you say began in the classroom, in one sense or the other?

At least one began as a literal course pack, though, right?

Which one?

Are you finally an artist or an archivist?

A creator or a collector?

Are you pro- or anti-appendices?

Did you write one draft all the way through?

Are you "anti-chapter"?

Do you posit a particular reader for whom you are writing?

When you're writing, are you trying to tap into the collective unconscious?

Care much anymore about an "audience"?

Do you care how posterity treats you when you're dead and gone?

A consummation devoutly to be wished for, huh?

Has this been a satisfactory exchange thus far?

What do you make of all this?

Where are we going with this?

Have you ever felt a truly intimate connection with another human being?

Do you see what I mean?

Ourselves

If we were not all so interested in ourselves, life would be so uninteresting that none of us would be able to endure it.

—SCHOPENHAUER

WHAT DOES IT MEAN to construct a self?

How do you write about yourself without becoming self-indulgent?

I.e., without spending too much time talking about trivial aspects of your life?

To what degree does your artistic project founder on the shoals of self?

To what degree are "humanity" and "self-reflexivity" synonymous?

To what extent, then, are we all also wrapped in the hoodie of selfhood?

Why do you come back over and over to the phrase "self-reflection in a convex mirror"?

Ashbery, right?

No?

Why do you come back over and over to the phrase "mirror turn lamp"?

Yeats, right?

Yes?

What's the point you're trying to get to?

Is yours a failed life?

A misdirected career?

Harold Brodkey, minus the hype?

The culture is now exceedingly weary and wary of its own astonishing narcissism and solipsism, and writers are self-critical about memoir in a way they hadn't been before—cause or result?

And you got caught badly in the backwash, wouldn't you say?

Because—is there even such thing anymore as a "self"?

It still exists?

Your former teacher John Hawkes spoke of "the terrifying similarity between the unconscious desires of the solitary man and the disruptive needs of the world." To what extent are you exhibit A?

In what sense are terrorists the new anti-novelists?

Are you a terrorist?

Are you sympathetic to terrorists?

How so?

Are you a self-terrorist?

Will you ever stop pummeling yourself?

Still not sure I get it. How, exactly, are you any more or less wounded, blind, flawed, wrong, doomed than anyone else?

Okay, but then how does the seemingly ceaseless prose-colonoscopy cast larger light?

Are you sure you're not looking through the wrong end of the instrument?

What's your favorite TV show ever?

Why don't you own a TV?

Oh, I see—you've "cut the cord"?

I'm very interested in this passage of Obama's because, in some way, it's through his reading that he begins to ask and answer the question "Who am I?" You've also done a lot of reading, so I suppose I'd like to ask you, who are you?

According to Georges Gusdorf, "Autobiography is the contest of a being in dialogue with itself." I wonder if you think such a formulation remains relevant, and if so, how?

Have you ever written anything that couldn't be interpreted as crypto-autobiography?

Why not, going forward, as an act of bona fides, publish your work anonymously?

Or only online?

Does not the perceiver, by her very presence, alter what's perceived?

Let's say you're writing a biography of Nathanael West, and while you're writing this book, a global pandemic occurs; would you keep your exclusive focus on West?

Or do the two tracks—"life and art"—somehow overlap and collide?

Is that possible?

Advisable?

Does your art constitute your entire life? If I were you, that would be my concern.

Is that the way you see your own writing?

As memoir?

As autofiction?

As book-length essay?

As self-demolition project?

As wannabe suicide note?

That is to say, when, pre-pandemic, you would be watching a movie in a theater (and perhaps even deeply enjoying the movie), you would continually be asking yourself if this behavior constitutes a valid human activity? That is so fucking weird.

How do you—or do you—ever break out of this wash-rinse-repeat cycle?

Are you truly as despondent as you claim to be?

Are you currently capable of taking any delight whatsoever in, say, Homer, Rembrandt, Mozart?

What, to you, is the definition of "genius"?

Is such a notion even relevant in post-postmodern society?

Have you read much attachment theory?

Ever really latched on to anything?

What matters to you?

Anything at all?

What is your go-to succor?

Your salvation?

Your damnation?

What do you want to get out of this interview?

You're asking what *I* want to get out of the interview?

Who's being interviewed here?

Who am I to say what belongs—is that what you're asking?

In or out?

David, can we please just try to be co-pilots here? That would be very helpful, from my perspective.

Childhood

Anybody who has survived his childhood has enough information about life to last him the rest of his days.

—FLANNERY O'CONNOR

WHAT'S YOUR BACKGROUND?

Yes, just in general—what is your background?

Where did you grow up?

What were your parents like?

Are they still alive?

Do you have siblings?

Were you raised in a religious family?

Standard, West Coast, deracinated, detribalized Jewish secularism?

This is a photo of the rather humble house in which you grew up?

You may be weary of this line of questioning, but why do you keep writing about the same material over and over?

You've now written at least two—and one could easily say more like several—books about growing up, more or less. Inevitable question: What gives?

You weren't raised in a gulag or Nazi Germany or by wolves. When are you going to grow up, some might ask?

Is there a sense in which your work is prima facie evidence of untreated PTSD?

Is this art or repetition compulsion, if you know what I mean?

"Essay" or therapy?

If you're claiming to recall something—verbatim—from fifty years ago, in what sense is it accurate to call this "true"?

Now, your father—he wrote for the *New York Herald Tribune*, right?

And your mother wrote for *The Nation*, right?

Were you as obsessed with the "Cyclops" TV column in *The New York Times* in the early 1970s as I was?

When did you realize that John Leonard was writing that column?

Didn't your cousin know him or something?

They worked together on the *Daily Cal* during the Free Speech Movement at Berkeley? Sounds so mythical.

Did Joan Baez really sing at your sixteenth birthday party?

You guys knew Tom Hayden and that crowd?

Mario Savio and his posse?

Alan Cranston—didn't your dad work for him briefly?

So, amidst Golden Gate Park anti-war demonstrations and flower power and R. Crumb and DROP ACID NOT BOMBS, where were you?

Who was little Davy Shields?

Card-carrying polemicist or incipient satirist?

Another way to say this is, your politics are a curious mix of lefty insurrection and rightist disdain—are you William Lloyd Garrison or William F. Buckley?

Are you hanging out or a hanging judge—get my drift?

Do you share with me a profound aversion toward everything Didion has become?

Was she an important influence you had to shed?

What influence if any were all the New Journalists you were assiduously reading in the then Bay Area–based *Rolling Stone*?

Hunter Thompson?

Joe Eszterhas?

Sara Davidson?

Et al.?

According to Paul Beatty, everything that has made life even slightly livable in the twenty-first century was invented on the West Coast. Do you think this is true or do you just love anything that animates in you the East Coast/West Coast cathexis?

You like to say you peeked behind the domestic curtain to spy a very vulnerable and weak Wizard of Oz—what does that mean, in a political context?

How, for you, is it somehow connected to Kundera and his rabid anti-Communism?

What mind of kid were you?

"Mind"?

Did I say "mind"?

What *kind* of kid were you?

Jock?

Basket case?

Both of the above?

What did your journalist-parents think of your becoming a writer, albeit one in curiously conflicted conversation with "journalism"?

Did they not live long enough to witness your transformation into a perpetual enfant terrible?

Were they proud of you?

Competitive in what sense?

Are you competitive at all with your daughter (whose graphic memoir I've read and like at least as much as anything you've done of late)?

Your father's name was Milton Schildkraut—that's for real?

That was his name until he changed it after the war?

Due to anti-Semitism or anti-German sentiment or both?

Do you see yourself as a German Jew?

A Jewish American?

Your mom's "maiden name" was really Hannah Rochelle Schevill?

Is your personality—to the degree you think of yourself having a quite specific one—closer to your mother's or your father's?

Your so-called work ethic—where does that come from?

How about your "humor"—Mom or Dad?

Whence the angst?

Could you see ever being able to flip that feeling (or perhaps lack of feeling) into something truly positive and productive?

I seem to recall one reviewer saying you "articulate and exemplify the endemic disease of our time—the difficulty of feeling." Touché?

Ever think you'll feel anything again for real?

Would you call yourself a troublemaker as a tyke?

If you hadn't become a writer, what would you have done?

Would you have survived the regimen required?

Is the Philoctetean wound-and-the-bow your single deepest narrative vector or only your most insistent?

Do you think that each of us becomes, in the end, pure persona?

Does anyone ever get beyond his own mask?

Mask upon mask? I get it.

Where do you fall, by the way, on the paranoia meter vis-à-vis covid? So far you don't seem to me insanely trepidatious.

Are you seeking an exit strategy?

How aggressively?

How self-destructively?

That incredible photo of you hitting the tape at the end of the 100-yard dash—where did all that light in your eyes go, Mr. Shields?

Speech

Are not our lives too short for that full utterance which through all our stammerings is of course our only and abiding intention?

—JOSEPH CONRAD

SO HOW BADLY *did* you stutter as a child?

Did you ever get to a point where you just wanted to throw up your hands and stop talking?

Stop writing, because language is the enemy, etc.?

And then, as you got older, of course, apparently yearn at times to stop existing?

Would you have become a writer if you didn't stutter?

Is stuttering the best thing to happen to you?

Are stuttering and stammering different?

Is it genetic?

Did either of your parents stutter?

Or is it psychological, mental, psychosomatic, environmental? Fill me in. I have no idea.

How did your family treat your impediment?

Was it worse for you when talking to girls?

Worse with pretty girls?

Worse with adults?

Worse still with authority figures?

Do you struggle particularly with consonants or vowels?

So the "problem sounds" migrate over time?

Right—like, how many different words do Eskimos have for "snow"?

What did you think of Michael Palin in *A Fish Called Wanda*? In real life, his father stuttered, as you may know.

How about Billy Bibbit in *One Flew over the Cuckoo's Nest*?

Billy Budd?

Anthony Blanche in *Brideshead Revisited*?

What are the other key stutter texts?

Is there a pattern, then, to how it gets portrayed?

You remind me a bit of the boy who can't swim but who jumps into the deep end of the pool to learn how; when your novel about stuttering was published, you went out and gave readings and did interviews. How did you conquer or at least manage your fear?

There's only the barest hint of a stutter when I listen to you now. Have you truly overcome it?

"Circumlocution"—that's the technical term?

What do you want the rest of us to comprehend about this baffling disorder?

Humans are the only animals who use spoken language to communicate; without it, we're the Elephant Man, aren't we?

Writing as revenge upon stuttering—how so?

Many writers are or were stutterers: Edward Hoagland. John Updike. Elizabeth Bowen. Somerset Maugham. David Mitchell.

Arnold Bennett. Lewis Carroll. Margaret Drabble. Budd Schulberg. Peter Straub. Nevil Shute. Kenneth Tynan. Machado de Assis. What do you see as the through line here?

"Aggressively minor"? Interesting.

Writing "fluently" about "disfluency"—how cathartic that must have been, I'm guessing?

You've written about how stutterers, in literature and in film and in life, often get away with certain rudenesses, certain violations, they wouldn't have gotten away with if they didn't stutter. What did you get away with?

Do you still?

Can I hear you read a little from the book?

How about the long paragraph at the end of chapter 5 about how "stutterers are the only truth-tellers; everyone else is lying"?

You doing okay over there, Mr. S.?

I'm going to press Pause, all right?

I thought that was fine, but perhaps you could read it one more time?

Don't you think we all have our own "speech problem," to some degree? I know I do.

Do you think anyone can really understand anyone else, and if not, what are any of us doing other than walking around trapped for eternity in our own space suits?

Reading

A writer is a reader who is moved to emulation.

—William Maxwell

Read any good books lately?

How much do you think about other people's work when you're writing your own work?

Do you believe in the book—the physical book—as a sacred object?

Has there ever been a better piece of tech than the book?

You're dating a librarian?

Seriously?

You're not just saying that, to make a broader point?

It's over now, though? Oh. Again, I'm sorry.

What is it you like so much about Cheever's journals other than, of course, his swooning self-abjection?

So, too, exactly the same with Katherine Mansfield's journals, right?

Pessoa's as well?

Same goes as well, I'm assuming, for Ernaux, Daudet, Fawcett, Julavits, Guibert, Levé, Michaels, Stendhal, Zambreno, Waldie, Trow, et al.?

You mean as works of art?

Are you in sync with Elif Batuman when she says she prefers most of her writer-friends' emails to the books they write?

Any sense of whether, following this widely disseminated remark (widely disseminated by you, I might add), she still has any friends?

Do you have any friends—real friends and not just colleagues or collaborators?

In your opinion, is there a way to feel good other than the pleasure derived from the articulation of sorrow?

Who if anyone will want to read this thing we're doing together here, especially during or even after the plague?

Is it a work of fiction?

Autobiography?

Staged debate?

Internal argument?

Crisis management?

Confession?

Documentary?

Socio-cultural intervention?

Suicide prevention hotline?

I don't see anything even slightly masked about it, do you?

Do you subscribe to Nabokov's assertion that the only necessary sexual toy is the mask?

What's the last book that "revolutionized human consciousness," to quote Mr. Mailer?

By how much?

I mean, does that even happen anymore?

How many readers share that fascination?

What's the harm in aiming to please the reader?

Kind of Freudian, isn't it?

What kind of books *do* you like?

Can you name one?

Do you, by chance, know Theodor Adorno's *Minima Moralia*?

Did you realize he wrote most of it in Los Angeles?

Not far from where you grew up? Huh.

All those German Jewish intellectual artist refugees who settled in LA—one of whom was, in a sense, your father, wouldn't you say?

Could you recommend some of Adorno's other books?

What is it about his work you like?

Oh, I see—not a big Frankfurt School guy?

Could you please name eleven prominent, contemporary writers whose work you vehemently dislike?

Why is that necessarily anathema?

"Write yourself naked, in blood, and in exile"—you seem to like a lot this line of Denis Johnson's, but what does it mean, in practical terms?

When you quoted it to that upbeat poet in your online conversation with her, I remember she blanched and took a step back, as if you were revealing more than you realized—did you read the moment that way, too?

The sadness of your self-imposed isolation?

Do you see Markson's last four books as attempts, somewhat belated and somewhat desperate and therefore immensely moving, to stake a down payment on his own "immortality"?

Which is total bullshit, right? So far, Shakespeare has lasted twenty generations, which is, obviously, the merest eyeblink. Everything vanishes.

You're not including *Wittgenstein's Mistress*, are you? I don't, either. That book doesn't work for me at all, *pace* Wallace's encomia.

What prevents anybody, including, most emphatically, you, from descending down the same rabbit hole?

Is it possible you're doing nothing more than documenting your private anguish and fobbing it off as art?

Are you copacetic with that?

How so for Woolf?

Didn't you once say you were actually utterly uninterested in even the *donnée* of *One Hundred Years of Solitude*?

A long, loud, entertaining, celebratory carnival of the human condition—not really your thing, is it?

Big fan of the Milosz line, aren't you—"I don't agree with the novel"?

You prefer the Olympian lamentation upon existence to the vivid evocation of existence, *n'est-ce pas*?

However, what's so bad about a work of fiction that features fascinating individuals and, through its depiction of their behavior, is implying certain things about the human condition?

You don't think that Ian McEwan and Elena Ferrante and Zadie Smith "embody contemporary consciousness"?

What does that even mean?

You don't really believe that, do you?

What's not to like about, say, *On Beauty*? I thoroughly enjoyed it.

Oh, really?

She thought so, too?

That was really her reply?

The Brautigan book?

In *Speak, Memory*—when Nabokov says, "I'm trying to remember the name, the name of the dog . . . and it's coming, it's coming, here it comes . . . Floss"—you don't really believe that, do you?

Why do we read a novel—to escape on wings of imagination, no?

What is your taste, then, in fiction these days?

You don't?

If George Eliot wrote *Daniel Deronda* to educate and entertain the upper-upper-middle class, we should all be deeply grateful for that, should we not?

You truly prefer Wallace's essays to his novels?

Not even his stories?

Not "Good Old Neon"?

Do you know his essay on Federer?

It's a suicide note barely and briefly avoided, is it not?

Is that why you like it so much?

Why does Quentin Compson kill himself?

Why don't you think of Nicholson Baker as a novelist?

Okay—a novelist per se, then?

In *Human Smoke*, he compiles and repurposes hundreds upon hundreds of very brief excerpts from newspaper articles, mainly from the *Times*, in order to make a powerful pacifist argument against World War II. Indeed, all war. What does that tell us about the possible purposes of pastiche?

In other words, is anything "original"?

He once said to you that if a book contains a single fudged fact, that makes it—ipso facto—a work of fiction?

Any book?

Without getting into moralistic notions, what do you make of what "JT LeRoy" did and how "he" built upon it?

Did "his" books not manage to accomplish something important?

Did they speak to you at all, as someone who deals with questions of truth-creep in memoir?

And "JT" really did send you that email? I love it.

Your aesthetic has changed dramatically over time, hasn't it?

How common is that, do you think?

To what degree might it be wise to attempt to reverse this slide?

Madame Bovary now bores you?

Hey, man; what else—*War and Peace*?

I hate to say this, but doesn't Dale Peck fit in here somewhere?

Whatever happened to him, anyway?

Aren't you and he friendly?

Do you have the same feeling about any book other than *In Search of Lost Time*—that you can no longer love something you once worshipped?

Are you ever happier than when you're reading?

Are you bored when you're not reading?

What's the matter with you?

No, seriously. What is your underlying impasse?

Why can't you feel?

What's buried beneath that seeming numbness?

Anything?

Have you read Grégoire Bouillier's first book, *Report on Myself*?

Reminiscent of what?

But what did she say? That's why I'm asking.

Do you have an example?

Did this happen to you?

How many people are actually going to read the kind of book you're adumbrating?

Any titles come to mind?

You'll email that list to me?

Do you have the hardcover with you, by chance?

Do you ever do this sometimes (especially when you're loving a book too much): start reading it back to front?

Melville praised Hawthorne for saying "No! in thunder; but the Devil himself cannot make him say yes." There isn't a lot of thunder in your orchestra, but your characteristic note is inevitably—seemingly without exception—"no." You good with that?

Perhaps you didn't get enough snuggles in the nursery?

No final, quasi-blistering aperçus?

School

It may be us they wish to meet, but it's themselves they want to talk about.

—Cyril Connolly

Is IT HARD to get into Iowa?

How hard, would you say?

One in ten?

One in a hundred?

Yikes. Are you sure?

Did you get in on your first try?

Where else did you apply?

Them again?

Didn't care to make your way in the big city?

What did you submit?

Was your fiction any good?

So you were in the workshop, then, and not the nonfiction program?

That wasn't even there then?

Do you think of me being a good fit for Iowa?

Do you think I could get in, based on that story of mine you workshopped and seemed to like?

Do you prefer a PDF or a Word doc?

Would you be willing to write a recommendation for me?

May I mark it as non-confidential?

Did you go to Iowa with anyone who became famous?

No one other than her?

I guess I meant famous famous?

How about among the faculty?

Was Vonnegut there?

Cheever?

John Irving?

J. P. Donleavy?

What is or was the Iowa method of teaching?

Does it work?

Is that a coherent pedagogy?

Do you still subscribe to it, would you say?

Who was the worst teacher you had during those two years in grad school?

How do you spell that?

Who was the best teacher you had?

Has she written any books?

Published?

Did you get a Teaching-Writing fellowship?

How about a postgrad Michener fellowship?

You lived in Iowa City for five years? Holy Moses.

Why?

I see—what has she written?

Anything else?

Was that hard for her?

For both of you?

Does it help that it's in the middle of cornfields?

It sort of forces people to concentrate on their work because there's nothing else to do?

You don't get cabin fever?

I've heard this line: "If you can survive Iowa, you can survive anything"—can you translate that for me?

Is there a certain type of person drawn toward this sort of self-renunciatory isolation?

What was the gestalt of your particular cohort?

What's the most helpful piece of advice you got at Iowa?

Least helpful?

What's your first reaction when you see someone wearing an Iowa Hawkeyes sweatshirt anywhere in the world?

How about a baseball cap?

Your first novel apparently came out of going to University of Iowa basketball games. Why didn't you write it as memoir, à la *A Fan's Notes*?

When you were in the workshop, you were also a patient in the university's speech clinic, "crossing a footbridge between two four-story brick buildings of language." Did the workshop faculty know you had a speech therapist, and vice versa?

Was Edward Hoagland teaching at Iowa then?

Did you and he ever talk about stuttering?

Would you have written your novel about stuttering if you hadn't been a patient there for five years?

Same question, I guess: if you wrote it now, would you write it as memoir, à la *Girl, Interrupted*?

What do you think—big picture—of those first two books of yours?

Twenty books later, do you worry about your graphomania?

Where's the fire, as they say?

Do you ever think of using a pseudonym?

"D. Jonathan Schildkraut"?

Seriously?

Is the graphomania related in some sense to stuttering?

How could it not be, I guess?

Do you now wish you had gotten a PhD so you could be discussing Roland Barthes on Racine rather than Brendan's confession re last night's debauch?

Are you a good teacher?

Are you "nice"?

I've seen some teaching evaluations for you online, and—to be honest—they aren't all that great. Any response?

I see—the proverbial pound of flesh?

I heard that Tin House said you couldn't come back because you were too mean toward your students. Is that true?

You also teach in a "low-residency" writing program. Is that legit or more of a soft scam?

Do you ever worry that you've contributed to a Program Era writing aesthetic?

Do you wish you taught in a writing program with a "nonfiction track"?

Why don't you?

That's on you, isn't it?

Who's the best undergrad you've ever taught?

Grad student?

Have you stayed in touch with Aaron Strumwasser?

Does writing still come fairly easily to you?

How about speaking?

I've seen some YouTube videos where your stutter got pretty bad—were you just nervous those nights?

Didn't take your meds?

I see—started upping the dose?

You were in grad school at the apex of "dirty realism"—Carver, Beattie, Frederick Barthelme, Mary Robison, et al. During that period, were you sympathetic or antipathetic to that literary movement?

How did it influence you, your work?

Are all your books available in paperback?

As ebooks, too?

How about in audio?

Could you quit teaching now if you wanted to?

Do you still like teaching?

Big fan of Zoom?

Any plans to retire soon?

Would you be terrified of the echoing isolation?

What advice do you have for when someone should start taking workshops?

For when they should stop?

I guess what I'm trying to ask is, exactly what are the tangible benefits?

Iowa is the oldest writing program in the United States; is it still also among the best?

You rarely mention that you went there; why not?

You're now in your mid-sixties. Have you accomplished what you wanted to accomplish?

Any inconsolable regrets?

If you had to write your obituary in exactly one hundred words, what would it say?

Knowledge

One night I sat for a long time at my desk in my study without doing anything at all until I suddenly began to beat myself about the head, I think in an attempt to make myself cry. I know I quite often wanted to cry, as if crying would bring release, but release from what? There was nothing to be released from. I wasn't in any pain. In fact, I hadn't felt so well, physically, for a long time, not for a couple of years. Knowledge, perhaps. Yes, it must have been knowledge that I wanted to be released from.

—SIMON GRAY

DO YOU WANT to live life or think about life?

It's not a rhetorical question; which is it?

Are you sure?

Was that sort of your epiphanic moment?

Is the overexamined life worth living?

By which I guess I mean, you've analyzed your life to death, but will you have lived your life at all prior to your death?

As you see it, what if anything is the difference between the truth that essayists supposedly seek and how, say, the *Times* sees truth ("The truth matters")?

CNN?

MSNBC?

Fox?

Trump?

Biden?

Can you define "truth"—preferably in one good long paragraph?

How about "imagination"?

What, in your lexicon, is history?

Where do we and where do we not need "scare quotes"?

Let's get down to it, then: How has the last century of modernism and postmodernism—subjectivity, relativity, Heisenberg's uncertainty principle, the contested space of "nonfiction," etc., etc.—paved the way, in a sense, for Trump?

To what degree are we all complicit?

To what degree are you more complicit than most?

You've written a screenplay about African American basketball players and directed a documentary about an African American football player. Does either project strike you now as being pretty problematic?

Does the reader of one of your books—or, for that matter, the viewer of one of your movies—depart with knowledge gained?

Wisdom gleaned?

Reversing field: What intellectual chaos have you helped create?

What epistemological shit have you blown up?

Is your goal in life to become blogger in chief?

Online disrupter?

Do you not worry that this approach and stance (the self-excavation ad infinitum, ad nauseam) can become—have become—unbearable not only for the reader but also for yourself?

Do you have a sense of that for yourself?

No one can put every relevant fact in; everyone chooses what to put in and what to take out. Surely the reader already knows this, does she not?

So every book is the potentially overbearing act of a would-be autocrat?

Did or did not FDR have polio?

Can we not settle on any facts whatsoever?

What's the difference between "facts" and "truth"?

What's the lifespan of a fact?

Where do you, personally, draw the line?

Can we please, please, please—not stop talking, please—but stop thinking about the world in precisely these binaries?

To what degree are you sympathetic to my framing of the argument?

Are you being characteristically pseudo-polite, passive-aggressively shy?

To what extent do you want or need to howl in anger?

You said that you like that Barry Hannah line—"At least the South can still howl"—but he's probably been canceled by now, wouldn't you think?

Can a biographer tell a kind of truth?

If so, what kind?

What kind of untruths—if any—can biographies engage in?

In this vein, what's your view of Edmund Morris's attempt to write an anti-biography of Reagan?

Dyer's of Lawrence?

McElwee's anti-biopic of General Sherman?

Another way to put it might be, what are the truths or untruths that biographers can tell?

How is this different from the truths and untruths that auto-biographers can tell?

Didn't Mary McCarthy cover all this quite completely last century?

Or, for that matter, Saint Augustine two millennia ago?

If everything can be disputed, what—as they say—is "real"?

Surely, this is Trump 101, but isn't it also Postmodernism 101?

Truth or dare, as they say?

Two truths and a lie, as they also say?

You struggled with that one, didn't you?

Remember spin the bottle?

Is there a more fraught game within the child's pantheon?

What I'm hearing you say, over and over, is that the real is nothing more and nothing less than how we interpret it. Yes?

Not exactly a new idea, is it, my friend?

When you say "entrenched," what do you mean?

Really?

Who truly knows?

So ... how do you get through the day if you "know" life is utterly bereft of purpose?

"When we are not sure, we are alive"—are you sure this is something that Graham Greene said?

Can you prove it?

Do you know what "JSTOR" stands for?

Toward the end of *Elizabeth Costello*, Coetzee affirms nothing about existence beyond the "joyous belling" of frogs that have risen up out of the mud after a long winter of hibernation, and you're saying that's more or less your "position"? Interesting.

"Everything is significant, but nothing is meaningful"—that's your default gesture?

That's just another quote from someone or other, though, isn't it?

Barthes?

Oh, John Barth?

In other words, where to start?

Whether to start?

Whether to end?

Truth

I refute it thus.

—SAMUEL JOHNSON

YOU GREW UP in LA and San Francisco in the 1960s and 1970s—surrealism central. Do you see that being a formative experience in the sense that, even now, for you everything is literally and figuratively "fugitive"?

"We try but cannot construct reality out of words." Yeah. Got it. But also sort of so what, though?

What is it we're seeking when we read a celebrity's ghostwritten Twitter feed?

I would think you would or should embrace the DIY ethos of the online writing communities that now, in a sense, dominate contemporary literary conversation, and yet you seem to view them askance. How can you justify that?

How do you think it will change writing in the future?

In your view, what is the origin of this current spate of "life writing"?

Yesterday, when I left the apartment, I noticed a guy who was (1) wearing a face mask and (2) taking a dump on the pavement. What do you say at that point—"Would you mind refraining?"

Why do you derive your deepest pleasure not from participating in your own activities but from viewing the activities of others?

But that's not a good thing, is it?

Any regrets on your part?

Children have legitimate "uses for enchantment," but adults don't, because we know we're going to die? That makes exactly zero sense.

Do you also intend to turn in your badge at some point soon, like the speaker in that Dylan song?

How do you mean?

Can you remember the last time in your life you were truly happy?

What counsel can you offer to a writer who would like to write about his own "damn, doomed life" but who's worried about the possibly deleterious consequences?

A form of procrastination? I see.

What work did you hope that book would do in the world, what "unacknowledged legislation"?

So: a mode of contemporary writing that's devoted exclusively to nerve-racking revelation, then. Okay—is that really what the reader wants, though?

It's more direct?

The interrogation is more viscous?

Or did you say "vicious"?

Oh—"visceral"? Better.

Do you think self-inquiry has become more prevalent as all of these mass (and massive) cultures threaten to shrink the self?

Isn't this just a simple matter of personal taste?

Can we please move on?

I'll text it to you; this is your phone number, right: 207-771-0733?

Due to covid, I'm thinking a lot of late about every writer's hyper-reclusion; the art and the artist are by definition distinct, for the nonce. Do you see any hidden value to this?

No more readings in bookstores? Woohoo.

Opening the aperture slightly, toward the end of this topic: Who's going to create the stories about our time that the world will remember?

The "internet famous"?

YouTubers?

TikTokers?

Who will watch these "works"?

Will we study them, as if they were Delphic ruins?

Who will own them?

But what is the role of the imagination in this "post-literature literature" that you envision?

Is reality really real, I guess I'm asking?

How can we enjoy memoirs, believing them to be true, when nothing, as we all know, is as unreliable as memory?

Who are you to criticize Beard in this realm?

Do you have any insight as to why she changed her mind?

Can I ask a question?

Have you ever looked for a long time into your own eyes in the mirror and seen how full of sadness they are?

Does the writer-self often interrupt or at least distract the self that's trying to be a husband, father, son, teacher, and friend?

How can we live our lives in the most serious possible way?

And this writer is you, trying to stay alive?

As Richard Price says, "The novel will be dancing on your grave." How could you possibly refute that?

Art

Life without music would be a mistake.

—NIETZSCHE

DOES FUN EXIST for you—I mean, in a contemporary context?

If writing isn't fun for you anymore, why are you still doing it?

What is fun, I guess I mean?

Do you know Jenny Gage's photographs?

Do you like them as much as I do?

Have you ever met her?

Do you study the placards in a gallery?

You don't "view" that as an act of not "seeing"?

Why do you choose a certain object to use in your art?

How do you choose that object—or that material, I suppose, is the way to say it?

How do you know you've chosen the right one?

Why do you repeat certain passages over and over?

Is this tendency just another instance of your impulse toward self-immolation?

What, if anything, does an artist gain by "revealing the mechanics" of a work of art?

Do you still think that, very briefly, in the early to mid-1980s, David Letterman was actually quite interesting?

Your book has many layers, of course, but isn't the crux of it a call to arms to fellow artists for a new art for a new century?

So what do you want?

Again, back to me, and what do *I* want?

There's no such thing as writing; there's only rewriting. It's very time-intensive. A book must be crystallized down to pure reduction. Are you still going through that refiner's fire?

If not, how can you call yourself a serious artist?

Should art have a point?

What is that point?

Shouldn't narrative art always be moving through time and space toward metaphor and, ultimately, meaning?

And here we come to "A book should either allow us to escape from existence or teach us how to endure it" (Samuel Johnson). I suppose I see where you would land here, with zero longing in the opposite direction?

How so?

You're talking about a certain kind of danger, correct?

Do you think of yourself as courting danger in your own work?

Really?

Compared with whom?

I suppose the inevitable response is to say, toward what larger purpose?

There's something achingly ancient in these arguments. What, for you, is the glitteringly new part? That's what I'm not seeing.

I guess I'm asking, what's wrong with the canon (even as it gets dramatically reconfigured year by year)?

And now (if we can even discuss these as antipodes anymore) "popular culture" has the whip hand and "high art" is apparently breathing its last; are you not surrendering too much here to the ambient noise?

Don't you worry that you're throwing out the bookbindery with the scummy bathwater?

Before we get to specifics—and you do have some quite specific ideas about what such work looks like—haven't writers been trying to get to and beyond the edge of art for centuries, even millennia?

Doesn't every generation produce its own misguided manifesto?

You say you heard a National Gallery tour guide "explain" that Rothko's "greatness" consists of how he forced artists who came after him to reconsider what they were doing. He changed the weather, etc. And this has apparently become for you some sort of gold standard—ludicrous, unreachable—for every work of art?

You've bet everything on "who would dare to believe he could pluck a single leaf from the laurel tree of art without paying for it with his life," and yet what if it's a diseased leaf?

Then what?

You're royally fucked, right?

What if the work, from first to last, is more or less DOA precisely because you cared about it too much—it and nothing else?

I'm thinking here a little of Kafka's "All I am is literature, and I am not able or willing to be anything else." Sad, in your case, isn't it?

You still love Rothko, though, don't you?

How about Diebenkorn?

Did you choose the cover? Very cool.

Rothenberg?

Why couldn't literature feel contemporaneous with visual art?

Why is literature thought to be unlike the other arts?

Why has that *derrière-garde*-ism only deepened over the last half century?

How many writers actually matter?

How many writers does it take to screw up the replacement of a light bulb?

Against the oncoming darkness, what consolation if any is the pseudo-immortality of art?

Brokenness

The only absolute knowledge attainable by man is that life is meaningless.

—TOLSTOY

DO YOU THINK of yourself as a random person?

You really do?

And that's where your brokenness gets accessed? I see.

Does that have anything to do with having a random rhythm?

By which I mean, I guess, is it related to your arrhythmia?

Not really any cure for that, is there?

Nor, exactly, for stuttering, is there?

You've learned to mitigate and ameliorate it, but that doesn't constitute a cure, either, does it?

More like a workaround?

What would you call it?

So you can't read a book that isn't shattered into caesurae of white space—why should that be of any interest to me?

I mean, what are the implications of that?

The connotation of such an emptying out?

What energy thereby gets dissipated?

Why do you read?

Why do you write?

Why are you doing this?

What's going to keep a reader reading?

Especially the contemporary reader, who has a million alternatives?

How about if we add—hey, here's an idea—a plot?

Will someone want to read it, without that?

So we're going to triple down on that idea?

That will be what we'll train our microscope on?

I want it to have genuine emotional power, don't you?

Do you think of yourself as an emotional person?

Where do you land on the "To those who think, life is a comedy; to those who feel, life is a tragedy" continuum?

Hence the remoteness?

Does life have a unifying force when viewed from thirty thousand feet?

Hence so many mini-sections, but where is the weave?

"Meaning," in your terms, is a matter of "adjacent data"? I see. I think.

Okay—no transcendental signifier; no universal design; how about at least an animating principle, a force field, an energy?

At most an herbarium of sorts?

Stuck in the same place for an awfully long time?

Not anywhere?

Not even in art?

That's quite a confession, don't you think?

Why wish?

Why not do it?

All very *Stroszek*, then, especially the ending with the dancing chicken?

What would be your rejoinder if I were to say that I find your (and his) stance almost completely unconvincing?

How has that changed for you over the course of your life?

It hasn't?

No one changes, improves, grows, "heals"?

Just "Vanity of vanities; all is vanity" and then "dust to dust" and then "Say good night, Gracie"? Yikes.

Failure

There is only one subject: failure.

—JOHN HAWKES

AS A WRITER, did you encounter any difficulty in the early going?

Did you ever feel like throwing in the proverbial towel?

What kept you going?

What keeps you going now?

Are you sure?

Did you do that standard thing of wallpapering your studio apartment with rejection slips?

You lived in New York during your twenties?

Your entire twenties?

Just south of Harlem?

What was that like?

It was affordable then?

Was Brooklyn happening yet?

Anything in particular gained from that experience?

For instance, did it help you find an agent?

A publisher?

Do young writers still need to move to New York—seems like such an old-fashioned idea in the internet age, don't you think?

Bury it beneath Schwab's Pharmacy?

Single most significant challenge you have had to overcome?

The medication has been helpful, then?

You're sure you're not overmedicating, though?

Do you agree that it tends to push you toward very high highs and very low lows?

Obviously, you've flirted with ideation in that direction, but how seriously? That's what I'm trying to get you to open up about.

Do you concur with Camus's observation that the only serious question is whether to commit suicide?

Was there any problem getting your first book published?

Was it as easy for you as it seems?

Do you ever think of removing your three novels from print now that you're so anti-novel?

Do you ever think of giving away copyright to all of your books now that you're so anti-copyright?

Was that your phone or mine that just buzzed?

Will you excuse me? I have to take this.

The cover on your second novel—good god. Did you have no say in the matter?

Are you still with them?

Are you capable of throwing a fit?

What do you imagine that might tell us about how deeply unhappy you really are?

Ever played good cop/bad cop with your agent vis-à-vis the publisher?

What was it that drove you to do that?

I'm wondering if that was conscious on your part—any sense?

Your alter ego protagonists in your three "novels"—all pretty much the same character, wouldn't you say?

They're all trying to work out their deepest problems through literature, always referring to some passage or another—remind you of anyone you know?

What strike you as your chief character defects?

Any character strengths?

None at all? Oh, please.

It can't be all that dire, can it?

Rhetorical question, I suppose, but are you more energized—in general—by other people (in which case you're an extrovert) or your own company (in which case you're an introvert)?

Have you been completely ensconced in your own little cubbyhole during covid?

Any other particular flaws that leap to mind?

What's the worst thing anyone's ever said to you?

That's awful, but I've heard worse, haven't you?

Embarrassing?

You felt embarrassed?

In 2014, I asked you what you meant by "necessary" work; you mentioned "cultural dread." Seven years later, can you build on that descriptor?

How has your most recent book been received?

In your view, what underlies the antagonism?

Can you unpack the pack mentality, I guess?

What did he call you—"labile"?

Did he find it guilty of sentimentality?

What is sentimentality, anyway?

Isn't that what is otherwise known as "feeling shit"?

So you can't communicate your essence fully, but, then, hey, who can?

Kind of comes with the territory, doesn't it?

That's an impossibly abstract and high bar, isn't it?

Can you provide at least a few examples?

Not to go all *Last Tango in Halifax* on you, but what do you imagine your main creative focus will be for you once you start receiving Social Security?

Any literary or cinematic magic left in your bag of tricks?

And the potential "greatness" of it would lie entirely in how you write it, would it not?

Will that happen?

Just as a human being, what is your goal over, say, the next decade?

Because, I agree—do we need more than the fingers of two hands to enumerate all the writers who have written a great book after age seventy-five?

In the short term, I agree; who knows?

Are you, in essence, a ghost?

Envy

It is not enough that I succeed; others must fail.

—LA ROCHEFOUCAULD

WAS GAYL JONES A GRAD STUDENT at Brown when you were an undergrad?

Did you ever meet her?

I wonder what happened to her; any clue? She was such a gifted writer.

Hawkes would always talk about Tournier and Yourcenar— did either ever do much for you?

Only the very ending of *The Ogre*?

I found his later books almost completely unconvincing because of the form they took. Do you think that's a legitimate criticism?

Walter Kirn says that some books are so bad they're good (we all know these), but also some are so good they're bad. They leave no room for the reader to breathe. If you agree with this formulation (and from your body language, you seem to be in vehement agreement), what are some examples for you of the latter?

So, too, nearly every work of *soi-disant* autofiction of the last decade?

Who are some of the most famous writers you know?

How awkward is it for you when they become more well known than you are?

Does the relationship fizzle out due to asymmetrical warfare?

Is that painful?

I'm not trying to bum you out—honestly just trying to pull back the proscenium curtain a little, if I may?

Bret Ellis?

Claudia Rankine?

Michael Cunningham?

Anyone else you used to know well?

Lorrie Moore?

Jonathan Lethem?

Maggie Nelson?

Cormac McCarthy—really? That's amazing.

These people still reply to your emails?

For example, Marilynne Robinson—one of my favorite writers. Obama's, too, for that matter. You say she writes Geritol prose. But isn't that just one (very envious) person's ill-considered opinion?

Do you still write blurbs for other writers?

Didn't you once try to put a stop to that practice for yourself?

How long did that last?

To me, the rule is that if you're going to adopt that policy, you can't then turn around and ask other people for quotes, don't you think?

What are you reading during all this downtime we now have?

Anything really blowing you out of the water right now?

Erika Menninger's first book? Haven't heard of it.

Do you read as a writer?

Do you know "Host," that essay Wallace wrote about a conservative talk show host?

"Because one can almost feel it: what a bleak and merciless world this host lives in—believes, nay, knows for an absolute *fact* he lives in. I'll take doubt." Uggh. So good, isn't it?

Have you ever been able to account for the curious elation you felt when you heard he had committed suicide?

Same when you heard about Kurt Cobain?

Or read about Plath, Sexton, Berryman, Hart Crane?

What is that all about?

I know you and Jonathan Raban are friendly. Any flareups?

Quibbles?

Quarrels?

Anything?

All sweetness and light?

David Milch was your teacher before he went on to write *Hill Street Blues*, *NYPD Blue*, *Deadwood*, etc. Would you say he had a huge influence on you?

Conventional in what sense?

So what?

Oh—"contentious," then, in what sense?

Dr. Chekhov's notion that the writer's role wasn't to prescribe but to diagnose: You find that a useful distinction?

All these fractal, gap-filled "texts" you write, read, teach, and champion—my sense is you're hoping to expand the definition of what might even be considered a book?

Where do Cha and Daudet fit in here?

Much of your work aims to be "transformative" in its "repurposing"—is that the way you try to frame it?

Your standard response is "Perhaps as many as half of the passages are 'mine,' though who knows what that means anymore," right?

I came across this comment on a blog somewhere: "David Shields is a dried-up hack who dresses up his acts of plagiarism with layer upon layer of bullshit. I pray for his fifteen minutes to be over." How do you deal?

Would you construct that book differently now?

"Your book has pierced and exploded my very heart"—have you ever had a reader say that to you?

If not, then what is the point?

Do you agree that the common denominator of melancholy, desire, regret, and jealousy is the glamour of absence?

Do you suffer from all these feeling-states to a staggering degree?

Do you commit the unpardonable sin of schadenfreude at least once a day?

Is your only regret that you're not someone else?

Jewishness

Jews don't drink too much. It interferes with our suffering.

—Milton Berle

Why do you think you were once so obsessed with Sandra Bernhard?

No, that's Sarah Bernhardt, isn't it?

Howard Schultz is Jewish, I assume?

Did you realize that anyone whose last name is the name of a large European city (e.g., London, Paris) tends to be Jewish?

What do we do with that info?

The rootless *cosmopole*?

You haven't attended services in more than thirty years, but you often name-check growing up in a left-wing, borderline red-diaper (pink-diaper?) Jewish family. Why mention it, though, if you're not going to explore it?

Reflected *engagé* glory?

When Leonard Michaels says that Kafka was never more Jewish than when he said he wasn't Jewish, what does he mean?

Recognize anything of yourself in that embrace and renunciation?

Henry Roth, say. Kosinski. Benjamin. Arendt. Proust. Koestenbaum. Babel. Adler. Levé. Markson. Gornick. Daitch. Spiegelman. You see the through line, don't you, quite beyond mere Jewishness?

Was Koufax everything to you as a kid?

That incredible California vanity license plate KFX 000—was anything ever better?

And even now you struggle to get proper distance on Israel, don't you?

I Would Have Saved Them If I Could—it's all right there in that perfect Michaels title, isn't it?

Didn't you meet his widow in Oakland recently?

Did you feel like a tertiary character in a Henry James novella?

All religious belief is, to you, utter nonsense?

Audience

She does not wave to the crowd, nor does she nod. She steps out of the limousine far enough for the door to shut behind her, and then she turns her face like a shield, and on it is written, "This is what you came to see." And then she goes in. I saw Joan Crawford with the naked eye, and she was *radioactive* with belief in herself. My image was *burned* on the wall behind me. Quite extraordinary. *Blazing*.

—QUENTIN CRISP

DO YOU FIND IT as odd as I do that nearly everyone in America knows who Ariana Grande is?

I mean, like, why?

Have you ever figured out what causes this?

When did this go from passing interest to mania?

Do you hold yourself above such manias?

How dangerous do you see it as being?

Is it possible to ever exit this spin cycle?

You've written books and now have made movies and have appeared on TV and radio shows and podcasts. Some people probably admire you. How do you handle it?

How does Julia Roberts?

I don't see even the slightest resemblance between you and John Malkovich, but you do?

Having a "big personality" or living a "big life"—are either of these things important to you?

Is it all right with you if I ask the questions?

Someone once described your first book of nonfiction as "*SeinLanguage* for highbrows"; do you see that as pejorative?

So it's one of these deals where the guy tries to be highbrow while talking about the lowbrow—"Here's how much I love Celine Dion," etc.?

Do you mean that you believe serious books aren't "entertaining" or that "entertaining" books aren't serious?

Oh, I see—"merely" entertaining?

All very Cynthia Ozick, isn't it?

Is that why Kirn no longer reviews for them?

Yes, yes, the pleasures delivered by mass culture, but at what cost?

At what weird, personal, self-hating cost do we purchase such ecstasies?

Am I completely out of bounds here?

So we're back to your own reflections on and in the media, but what makes your book different from countless other critiques of mass culture, going back to at least McLuhan if not Plato?

I'm sorry—am I boring you?

It's a boring question, maybe, but I was wondering, as a sort of starting point, how writing the book in Los Angeles affected you?

You often liken your "collage" work to "film editing"—how much of your formal approach is influenced by the California media world?

By the fact that you grew up in LA and San Francisco?

Where does Oprah—now ensconced, of course, in Santa Barbara—figure in all this?

Is she a useful model for you?

You haven't been influenced by her in any way?

Not even your impulse toward confessionality?

In this election year, do you have any comments about image and celebrity in the realm of politics in our country?

Have books had as much of an influence on you as film and TV and music and stand-up have?

The Wire, say—is there an American novel that has come within a hundred miles of that show in the last two decades?

In that case, why do people keep writing books?

A meme often comes from completely anonymous sources and relies entirely on the topical relevance of its subject matter. It uses entertainment that's been fed to the masses and then retools it in a subvert-the-dominant-paradigm sort of way, and it has real origins, albeit an "anonymous creator." Is this a new path?

I mean, in the age of the internet, what do you do now?

Is this a common query among your students?

What if anything is the value of writing and reading in a digital world?

Can you imagine what, you know, Whitman would do with the web?

Or Joyce?

Why produce something as antiquated as a book?

What's your take on the cut-up folks—Burroughs and Acker— and to what extent were they an inspiration for you?

Way before the pandemic, there are countless examples of your investment in distance and remoteness. Did popular culture and its remote apparatuses make you this way?

Contrariwise, you're driven toward "all that space that is the space between us"; hence your attraction to the mechanism of mass media and its inaccessible icons?

How did it feel to go on a media tour (when people still did such things!) on which you were expected to talk about the remoteness of media?

How meta was that?

I can't even remember, can you?

Why would that still be central to the culture now, though?

Like, if you had to name a single album that you adore, what would you say?

And the internet killed that as well?

It's all very "the work of art in the age of mechanical reproduction," then?

What did you once love?

So you're not looking down your nose at pop culture?

You share my love of Garfield the cat?

It's rather like arguing against oxygen, isn't it?

As in, "Are you opposed to the very air we breathe?"

Do you like breathing?

Yes or no?

Capitalism

Capitalism is the astounding belief that the most wickedest of men will do the most wickedest of things for the greatest good of everyone.

—JOHN MAYNARD KEYNES

HAVE YOU EVER HELD any of these jobs, and how quickly were you fired from each of them—

McDonald's parking lot attendant?

Stock clerk at a fabric store?

Stock boy at a car stereo outlet?

Didn't you once nearly die when you fell from the rafters?

Dawn custodian in women's freshman dorm?

Afternoon custodian in grad center?

Ever swept out the Augean stables?

Locksmith's apprentice?

Proofreader at greedhead law firm?

Transcriber of a Revolutionary War general's diaries?

Were you credited at all in the acknowledgments?

Teaching assistant to someone named Girlie Meta?

Teaching assistant for someone named Florence del Presta?

Bookstore buyer?

To what degree if any do you blame the publishing industry for our culture's need to find and fit ever smoother pegs into ever rounder holes?

Have you ever paid, implicitly or explicitly, for "sexual services"?

What does that mean?

What do you think of the market-driven memoirists who dot the American literary landscape?

Are you in artistic league with them?

Have you ever been thrown out of an NPR affiliate in Brattleboro, Vermont?

Have you ever been thrown out of an indie bookstore in Bolinas, California?

Why?

That was the question you asked at both places?

Whatever happened to Dave Eggers?

You used to be friendly with him, right?

Now would you say he's well on his way to becoming as tirelessly, tediously, and uselessly earnest as Wendell Berry?

All this by way of prelude to asking you whether McSweeney's is solidly in the black, and if not, why did you go with them for that book you wrote or co-wrote about porn or sexual abuse or whatever it was?

How much money have you made from all your books?

That former student of yours got a million-dollar advance for that book of hers. Have you read it?

How did you like it?

How jealous are you of it and her?

Oh, $2.5 million—really?

Any good?

In any case, have you made that much in your entire life from all your books?

If your books aren't really selling anymore—which more or less means that you no longer have a readership—then why, exactly, are you still writing them?

I honestly don't mean to goad you; I mean this simply as inquiry: Do you flatter yourself that your work is altering the culture in some subtle, incremental way?

That it's "high art" or avant-garde praxis or theoretical intervention or whatever, and over time it may alter somewhat the aesthetic of the next generation?

That's the age-old hope, isn't it?

I can see how a visual artist such as Rothko might think this way, but how does it apply to writers?

Your attempts to surmount or supplant what literature is and always has been—a more or less linear narrative about recognizable human beings—are perhaps well intentioned and energetic but also sort of irrefutably wrong. Can you push back against me here at all?

Where does poetry fit in all this?

Dickinson?

Kafka?

Melville?

André Gide turned down *Swann's Way*, did he not?

T. S. Eliot turned down *Animal Farm*, did he not?

How much money does the Federal Reserve destroy each year—any guess?

Why does it do that—any clue?

Are you good at math?

You enter a convenience store and hand the clerk a twenty to pay for fifteen dollars' worth of gas. The clerk hands back to you three fives. You don't discover the mistake until you're driving off. What do you do?

Or: You have two objects. One is worth a dollar more than the other, and they are worth $1.10 total. How much is each object worth?

You stand in front of doors A, B, and C. Behind two of the doors are goats, and behind one is a car. You pick door A. The announcer goes to door B and opens it: it's a goat. He asks you if you want to take door C or keep door A. Should you switch doors?

You're not very logical, are you?

Is your net worth substantially more than a million dollars?

Are you worth more dead than alive, Jesse James?

I never got why Franzen was so ambivalent, or pretended to be so ambivalent, about Oprah's benediction, did you?

If she called me, I'd answer on the first ring, wouldn't you?

I mean, I suppose she no longer has her book club anymore; is there a current equivalent? I suppose not.

I guess what I'm getting at is, is there is a way to see your work as, in a sense, self-help-adjacent?

Life, death, reconciliation, the peace that passeth understanding, etc.?

Just think of some of their titles—very emo, as we said earlier. Do you ever think of downshifting, ever so slightly and subtly, as a way to enter a much more commercial realm?

I mean, didn't someone or other compare one of your books to Kahlil Gibran's?

You're there, but you're not?

Tantalizingly close?

My father-in-law has two tickets to the Super Bowl. Excellent seats. Lower bowl. Forty-yard line. All expenses paid. Invited me. Where are you watching the game?

Paternity

Man is weak, and when he makes strength his profession, he is weaker.

—ANTONIO PORCHIA

SO YOU'RE A SON, obviously, but you're also a father. Do you agree that all male writers are finally either sons or fathers?

For example, Thomas Mann was a father; Kafka was a son—see what I mean?

Or Obama saying that all men are trying either to win their father's admiration or overcome their father's mistakes—where do you fall in the patrilineal lineup? Obama said he was doing both, of course.

You have only one child—is there a cruelty involved in such a decision?

A selfishness, I suppose is what I mean?

How do you and your daughter get along now that she's twenty-eight and an accomplished memoirist in her own right?

In this regard, how easy is it to swallow a bit of your own medicine?

Where does she live now?

How about you?

Primarily in your own head, I'm venturing?

What sort of parent was your father?

He was in and out of mental hospitals your whole life, is that correct?

Thirty-three shock treatments over ninety-nine years—almost impressive, in a way, isn't it?

Do you see yourself inheriting his bipolarity to any degree?

Is that why you take such a high-powered SSRI, to ward off the demons?

Does your daughter ever worry that the bipolarity has skipped a generation?

How do you deal with that worry on her part?

Are you close to her, would you say?

What sort of father are you compared with your father—please tell me not equally AWOL?

How is that going—your new relationship with your half-brother, whom you barely knew until you were fifty?

When your dad died, did you cry?

Why not?

But you did go through a weird psychosomatic illness at that time—some sort of high fever?

Do you and your half-brother compare notes on your father from different points of view?

How old was your father when you were born?

Was that über-awkward—people thinking he was your grandfather?

How have you tried to make amends for that?

How old were you when your daughter was born?

Same age as you—your ex-wife?

Your thirtieth anniversary would have been next year—what gemstone is associated with the event if the couple is divorced?

Are you aware that your daughter identifies herself on her Instagram page as "kinda jock, kinda emo"?

Ring any bells?

Do you have a theory of fatherhood?

A telos, I suppose I'm asking?

What do you think of Borges's view that to replicate oneself via paternity is an act of vulgarity?

Do you find the truism true—children never want to read their parents' books?

Any explanation for this phenomenon?

To me, "father" means distracted; what does it mean to you?

"Vacancy"? Yoiks.

How did you react when the Dutch translator of your second novel asked you if "Daddums" meant "molten fool"?

Would you call your father a man of letters, journalist, ad man, publicist, gun for hire, or hack?

Shit My Dad Says is disposable piffle; why do you persist in praising it?

How did you avoid serving in Vietnam?

But you still registered as a conscientious objector?

"A part of me has been born that never would have been born if I hadn't had the chance to gaze at my infant child"—can you react, please?

Are you in a sense addicted to crisis or at least tension, and how have you avoided (if you have) passing this tendency on to your daughter?

Oh, I see—a "blunted affect"?

I suppose what I'm asking is, have you escaped the liar's paradox or narcissist's dilemma?

Do you hate or love Schopenhauer's dictum "The truth shall prevail, though the world perish"?

How about you—how badly do you want to perish?

To what extent, if any, do you gild the lily when speaking to your daughter?

Do you discuss these issues with other men, other fathers, other writers?

Is love the answer?

Games

There is more wisdom in your body than in your deepest philosophy.

—Nietzsche

So is it kind of a DFW-type thing—you were an ordinary schoolboy athlete and now pretend you were once a physical marvel?

What were you so good at, then?

Oh, I see. You were really fast?

How fast?

Really?

What were your main sports?

But you were very short and slight until age sixteen?

Then what happened?

Your broken leg—kind of a convenient excuse, don't you think?

It's not as if you were destined to be Seabiscuit and then, after the broken leg, you suddenly became Stephen Hawking, is it?

What did you learn from it all?

There's that hoary cliché about how sports teach people focus and hard work and discipline; you're not going *there*, are you?

What would you say to those of us who have never picked up a croquet mallet or hockey stick?

First, track; then baseball; then basketball; then tennis; and now what, Mr. Shields—spectator sports, I guess?

You played freshman basketball at Brown, right?

Or tried out for the team?

Scrimmaged with the JV?

Attended a few games?

Waved a few pompoms?

"Pompons"? Not sure I follow.

What sports do you play now?

Swimming—does that count?

A little table tennis?

Power-walking?

Leaping to conclusions?

Your father was a part-time sportswriter—seriously? That's too perfect.

What influence did that have on you?

When that one review called you a "sportswriter," what was your reaction? None too pleased, I'm guessing.

And yet the only movie you've made so far is about a sports personage, right?

If I were to watch a game with you, would you have "better eyes" than I have?

What do you see about, say, ice hockey that I don't?

Are you one of those annoying people who call out the play five seconds before it happens and then gloat about it to the assembled multitude?

What was your reaction to Super Bowl XLVIII?

Super Bowl XLIX?

I would argue that all scopophilia is by definition meaningless. Watching other people play a game, though, strikes me as being at the extreme far end of meaninglessness. How do you justify it?

Or do you feel no such need?

A few of your books deal with the rapture of fandom. Why do you write so much about vicariousness?

I mean, why is that a topic worth writing about?

Is fandom not a form of self-humiliation?

Kind of your go-to *topos*, wouldn't you say?

Do you still watch sports?

Are you grading papers and checking your email while you're watching the game, or are you really "concentrating"?

What's your favorite game now to play or watch?

Did you once really sink twenty-seven consecutive free throws?

Any witnesses?

Is it depressing to live in a city that has such bad sports teams?

Which teams do you follow?

Do you miss the Supes?

What is the likelihood they'll return?

Do you have any "inside dope"?

Is that why you're saying that?

What's the point of publishing a book about a team's nondescript season so many years after the season?

Your press credential was revoked, so you had to buy a front-row season ticket?

How much did that cost?

And you lied to your then-wife about how much the ticket cost? Fascinating.

Did that lay down a marker that got played finally and fully in your divorce many years later?

Do you feel excited about the upcoming season, despite all the precautions?

Can YouTube videos of gorgeous plays still give you the chills?

Which ones come to mind?

Exactly—that time he did a somersault into the end zone?

We Average Unbeautiful Watchers—great title, isn't it?

Who wrote it?

Have you read it?

Do you plan to?

What other fan narratives do you like?

You a fan of fan fiction, by the way? Just curious.

You wouldn't name-check Nick Hornby?

Why not?

How about Frederick Exley?

C. L. R. James?

Bill James?

Anyone else?

You sure we can't shoehorn Hornby onto this list?

What did Lute Olson think?

George Raveling?

George Karl?

When Bret Ellis told you that his deepest wish was to be Tom Brady, how seriously did you take him?

Do you ever need to take a break from sports?

I suppose the last year or so has been that self-enforced hiatus, hasn't it, due to the virus?

Someone told me you can do the breaststroke all the way across the pool underwater without coming up for air—true? Cool.

What is your fastest time in the 100-meter freestyle?

"Fame is a vapor, popularity is an accident, and money takes wings. The only thing that endures is character." Why did David Halberstam use this as the epigraph to *The Breaks of the Game*?

Why did OJ love the quote so much?

A teensy bit ironic, in retrospect, isn't it?

Why do you love the quote so much?

Are you yourself a person of sterling character?

We're all hoping, right?

Is that a key relationship for you—between language and sports?

What was it John Hawkes said to you, just before you graduated—that everything you write is about "the agony of love without communication and in the context of violence"?

How did you/do you deal?

How large a part does insecurity play in our culture?

Don't you think this undergirds such phenomena as the mass watching of others?

If I can feel like . . . whoever . . . or look like . . . whoever, I won't have to feel so shitty about myself. Right?

And if that's true, does this participation in memoir and "truth" culture not equate with a larger drive to discover if others are as "needy" as we are?

"We are all so afraid; we are all so alone; we all so need from the outside world the assurance of our own worthiness to exist." It's all very Ford Madox Ford, isn't it?

Or, pivoting back to the departure point, you say, "Athletes are in touch with the gods; that's why we love them." Have you ever talked to an athlete and asked if he or she was willing or able to entertain the idea that he/she was indeed in touch with the gods?

"Pivoting" is a big sports word, right?

Did I finally get one sports term correct? Yay.

Any current player on whom you have a major crush?

Why do you put these feelings (of love, of idolization, of rapture, of perfection) on a pedestal?

Is there not another kind of love (more earthbound) you might privilege instead?

Is it that hard for you to accept your own human imperfection?

Why?

Dostoevsky: "I maintain that hell is the suffering of being unable to love." Is fandom, therefore, maybe something you need to overcome?

Coaching

You have to be smart enough to understand the game and dumb enough to think it matters.

—PETER GRIFFIN

WOULD YOU CLASSIFY YOURSELF as a stage parent—over-invested in your child's success?

Did you ever coach your daughter's soccer or basketball teams?

What in your view makes for a good coach?

A good teacher?

Is a good writer by definition a bad teacher and vice versa?

Are you a bad teacher?

A good teacher?

A good enough teacher?

A good enough teacher, in the Winnicottian sense?

Prefer undergrads or grad students or adults?

When you played doubles on your high school tennis team, did you suffer from what Wallace said he suffered from—a "bad head"?

Are there bad heads and then really bad heads?

Is there a sense in which you're all too sane?

Didn't Joe Wenderoth, of all people, once call you refreshingly normal?

Do you subscribe wholly to the Flaubertian dictum to be a bourgeois in life so you can be a radical in your art?

Do you share my contempt for Greenpoint hipsters who look and act cool but whose work is about as challenging as a Toblerone bar?

Did you ever study with Gordon Lish?

What did he like about your bracelet-cum-watch?

Do you model yourself after his teaching style?

If not Lishian, perhaps more Hawkes-like?

Are you more of an encourager?

A coach, for lack of a better term?

A mentor?

A cheerleader?

Comrade?

Companion?

Older brother?

Tough-love shrink?

Is the entire workshop model an obsolete one, and if so, have you not benefited from a model that is not only deeply authoritarian and patriarchal but also inherently racist, misogynistic, and anti-democratic?

Why didn't you reinvent the pedagogy?

Oh, you did?

You count that as reinvention?

How do you offer suggestions to students about their work?

Via marginalia?

Email?

Office hours (pre-covid)?

Macro critique or more micro?

Are you honest?

Searingly honest?

What, to you, makes a great coach?

Who's the greatest coach you've ever had?

Do you recognize "fake hustle" when you see it?

Do you know who coined the phrase?

Have you ever relied on a TA?

Does he mark up the papers?

Ever wish you'd married Véra Nabokov?

Do you ever read aloud student work in class?

Show doc films in doc film class?

All the usual tricks?

How exciting is it to see students making exactly the same mistakes on page 17 they made on page 1, the same mistakes at the end of the semester they made at the beginning of the semester, the same mistakes they make now they made forty years ago?

Weird to still be teaching?

In this vein (same mistakes after forty years), how hard is it to root for the Mariners?

Ever wish you'd gone to law school instead?

Why do right-wingers love baseball, Jews love basketball, and MAGA types love football?

What did Mary McGrory mean when she said, "Baseball is who we were; football is what we have become"?

Can a work of art still make you cry?

If not, why bother?

Why bother doing anything, then?

I think of the old joke about "so-and-so dying—but who could tell?"

Paging D. Shields?

Response, please?

I know we're not supposed to quote Woody Allen anymore, but what do you make of his claim that he's never been as riveted by a work of art as he is by game 7 of an NBA championship series?

To drill down a little further now: How, exactly, do you view your role as a teacher?

Do you ever feel like just saying, "Fuck it—send in the clowns"?

You've had several great teachers, an equal number of awful teachers, and many in the middle; objectively, where do you rank yourself?

Objectively?

Do you truly extend yourself as a teacher?

Do you view the classroom as an existentially vital space?

I guess I mean, do you view the classroom as spiritually holy?

Yes, of course, physical distance during the pandemic, but in normal times do you keep psychic distance between yourself and your students?

In a necessary way or a quite egregious way?

When, post-vaccine, will you return to the classroom?

Ever taught a truly great course?

How about a single really excellent class?

How about a genuinely meaningful one-on-one conference with a student?

Perhaps you view teaching as nothing more than a day job?

A sinecure?

What's your salary?

Seriously?

Seems to me a poor expenditure of taxpayers' dollars, since what do the residents of the state actually get as a result?

Can you think of any great coaches who were great players?

They don't easily come to mind, do they?

Why are all the great coaches ex-journeymen at best?

Could a great analyst have never played the game?

So you *do* bet on the games, then?

Did she know how much money you bet and lost on the Sonics that year, and was that a contribution to the early erosion of the marriage as well?

If students are really struggling with basic syntax, do you just outsource the task of remedial instruction to the writing center?

You now have a lot of Chinese nationals as undergrads, and their written English is far from perfect, so how do you handle that geopolitical issue?

Ever had that blow up in your face?

What's the scariest experience you've ever had in class?

Did you call 911?

How did the police handle it?

Ever wish she'd just gone ahead and pulled the trigger?

Best question you've ever asked in class?

Been asked?

Is there such a thing as being overprepared for class?

For a game?

What is just the right amount?

I want you now to carefully contemplate whether it may be a fireable offense—your overreliance on those three anthologies that you've co-edited. Well, is it?

You teach those in all your courses, I gather, and thereby earn a pretty penny, I would think?

What would happen if I reported you for using those anthologies? I have to say I find that very problematic, David.

Isn't "anthologist" the last job title before "deceased"?

Do you find that you stutter much anymore in class?

How about when you're badly underprepared?

How about when there is a woman in the class who has "the look"?

Is it true that in your very first class—as a TA at Iowa in the fall of 1979—you walked into the room with your zipper down and then, trying to quickly zip up, wound up spilling all your change onto the floor?

Could you laugh about it at the time?

Certainly now, though, right?

Why does teaching so exhaust one—physically?

Just as coaches get all sweaty on the sideline, do you also wind up sweaty and depleted?

It's weirdly sexual, isn't it, in a way?

At least pre-covid, you seemed to travel a lot during the school year; did someone cover for you?

How did that work?

Do you have a deep bench—an effective assistant coach or two?

How do you attempt to position yourself vis-à-vis the entire morass of identity politics?

Ever been called out?

Called onto the provost's carpet, as it were?

Canceled, literally or figuratively?

What is your single biggest regret about that visit of yours to Shaperson State University?

That whole remix you did of sports clichés—can you give me some examples? I don't "speak sports," as you well know.

Greatest sports accomplishment of your life?

Most memorable game you've seen live?

Ever seen a no-hitter?

Does any of that stuff still register?

Seems awfully childish, doesn't it, for someone of your supposed "seriousness"?

Best coaching/teaching you've ever done?

When your daughter scored the goal to win the city soccer championship, why could you not stop crying?

Really?

I think of you as very interior, very introverted. Do you consciously adopt a persona in class?

Do your students still surprise you?

If not, then, really, WTF, David?

So…most of your students' *parents* are now at least a full decade younger than you are. How do you bridge the pedagogical gap?

Let's say I told you that you had to retire right now. What would be your immediate reaction?

Can you please stop doing that?

Do you prefer students who blindly worship your every utterance?

Is that why students laugh so much at your jokes in class?

It gives one a false sense of comic bravura, doesn't it?

Could you email me every syllabus you've ever created?

Do you mind? I'd like to conduct a metadata analysis.

Is there such thing as a teachable book that's not a good book?

Are your books teachable?

Are they good, in your opinion?

Are any of them very good?

Have you ever fantasized about winning the Nobel Prize in Literature in the year 2040?

You would be—what—eighty-four?

Strike you as being very likely?

More likely than winning the Nobel Prize in Physics?

What makes a great writer or athlete?

What precise combination of gift, focus, passion, discipline, hard work?

You've written profiles of many prominent athletes and coaches; what did you learn?

Kobe Bryant once referred to the "awfulness of greatness." What does that mean?

Do you perhaps lack precisely this quality?

Has anyone you've interviewed ever turned his back on you?

Threatened you with a baseball bat?

Accused you of lying?

Is character fate?

Is that what connects sports and art?

For example, Pete Carroll overcorrecting and once again blowing second-and-goal from the one?

For another example, your becoming the kind of writer your parents would both applaud and deplore?

Seem strange to you that your father only ever criticized you to your face but only bragged about you incessantly to everybody else?

That your mother never hugged you except the day you got accepted into three Ivy League schools?

What is the perfect blend of freedom and discipline—in a work of art and in an offense?

If the triangle offense has potentially magical properties as a basketball strategy, what has similar value for writers—perhaps so-called freewriting?

Collage?

"Just shooting a lot of film," as you would say?

Literally or figuratively?

Would you classify this interview as a learning experience?

Athletic competition?

You seem to collaborate a lot with your former students—even very recently graduated students. Is this proper?

Ethical?

Legal?

Child abuse?

Vampirism?

Bullying?

How would you define success?

Failure?

In art or sports?

"The cemeteries are full of indispensable men," as de Gaulle said, so what does any of this matter?

Rilkean—in what sense?

But you're too old to change your life in any substantive way, wouldn't you agree?

So—not to put too fine a point on it—has it been a wasted life?

Criticism

All criticism is a form of autobiography.

—Oscar Wilde

Is THAT SOMETHING you still do—read all your reviews?

Every last word of every one?

Both positive and negative?

Really?

Why?

Are you unusual in that regard?

Didn't you once look up every bad review of your first several books and quote the meanest lines?

What was up with that?

Do you see that as a not very subtle form of masochism?

I guess what I'm asking is, how much do you hate yourself?

Do you see a way going forward to mitigate and finally empty out that emotion?

Is the relationship between every critic and every writer sado-masochistic in essence?

What is that Conrad story called, "The Secret Sharer"?

Is that not every critic and every writer?

Is there a sense in which most critics try to use most writers as a way to "get well," pretending to be healthier than the putatively ill human who committed the crime of writing the book?

Who was it who said, on the basis of one of your books, that your then-wife should divorce you?

How could that not lodge indelibly in her psyche?

Karinsky's one reservation about your second novel was that it was too nakedly autobiographical. Do you think that's a fair criticism?

He also wanted less contemplation and more narrative, more scene. You more or less concur, don't you?

You haven't published any reviews in a very long time. Why not?

No takers?

No invites?

Are you too much of a "loose cannon"—a man without a country, so to speak?

Do the best reviews alter your understanding of what you've written?

What's the smartest review you've ever received?

Did you write her to thank her?

What's the stupidest review you've ever received?

What do you mean, how much time do I have?

What's the most vitriolic review you've ever received?

Perhaps you can file a lawsuit when someone says something like that?

What do you do when people get basic information wrong?

Do you write a letter to the editor?

Do these ever appear in print?

Is there a sense in which nearly every book you've written over the last twenty years can best be understood as a poison dart aimed directly at the "literary establishment"?

Does such a thing still even exist?

Is there another sense in which nearly every book you've written over the last forty years can be best understood as a poison dart aimed directly at yourself?

Do you ever take your books-in-progress, show them to other writers for "feedback," and then revise the work based on their suggestions?

Who has been your most useful "first responder" in this sense?

The most unhelpful?

What's the worst thing a reviewer can do?

Have you ever imagined killing a critic?

Isn't there a Stoppard play that does that?

Doesn't he get mainly good reviews, though?

Is one reason you love Simon Gray's *Smoking Diaries* so much because he can't stop worrying the sore tooth of bad reviews?

What are the kinds of reviews that infuriate him?

Infuriate you?

Did you ever meet him?

Didn't you briefly get to know his widow?

Do you know anyone who knows her?

Could I trouble you for her email?

Is it true that you once outlined a book about Michiko Kaku-tani that was going to be called *Limning the Chiaroscuro* and was going to remix every review she'd ever written?

Oh, I see—those were her two favorite words, and she used them over and over?

Well, we all have our go-to vocab, don't we?

For instance, for you, the following words: "candor," "brave," "meditation," "rigorous," "excavation," "examination," "explora-tion," "investigation," "relentlessly," "bottomlessly," "powerfully," "enormously," "human," "animal," "text," "intimacy," "urgency," "existence," "sex," "violence," "metaphysical," etc., etc. Pot/kettle/ black, mister?

Is that the point, for you, of Markson's compendia of ludicrously "wrong" reviews of books now worshipped?

When I google you, thumbnail photos come up of other writers I've never heard of, like Thomas Ligotti. Any clue why?

Has the praise so far, in your forty-year career, reached the level of your expectations?

Nothing could ever fill the void, could it?

Suicide

Suicide is painless.

—MICHAEL ALTMAN

WHY IS THE HUMAN ANIMAL so sad?

Why are we so melancholy?

How can we ever come to live with loss?

How do we ever reconcile ourselves to the ultimate loss—the loss of our own life and the lives of our loved ones?

Yes, of course, sans any sort of religious mumbo jumbo; that's implied, isn't it?

What did you do with the people placed in your path?

What did you do with the people in your life?

Did you love them?

Did you show it?

Did you demonstrate it?

Were you there for them?

Were you emotionally available?

Isn't there a guy named Shields, I kid you not, in eastern Washington, who has kept the longest or longest-running diary, endless accounts of everything he does all day?

Going back to the idea that autobiography and memoir are about the remembered life—what *is* a remembered life?

What, after all, is any of us going to remember?

. . . Or are we going to be remembered for?

In your opinion, what is the best way to die?

I've always liked the phrase "die in the saddle," but what does it mean, exactly?

Is it exclusively double entendre?

Do you find that aging changes things with regard to this question of mortality?

Just the fact that you saw your best friend die and didn't handle it well?

Relatively recently, you had to deal with your father's very gradual decline and death. Did he not know how to enter that final stage?

Was he awaiting instruction?

Some sign from you, perhaps?

Did you feel bad that you weren't at his bedside when he succumbed?

You find this in Epicurus, Lucretius, Spinoza, all the Stoics: "Death is nothing." Everything that is . . . is sensation; the absence of sensation is nothing; death is the absence of sensation. Therefore, why worry about death?

It's seeing the skull beneath the skin, isn't it?

As Eliot said of Webster, obsession with death is a gift, or burden, of temperament, don't you think?

Why is the adolescent imagination so morbid, so death-shadowed, so suicide-haunted?

It can't all just be chalked up to *The Sorrows of Young Werther*, can it?

I don't know if there's a lot to be derived from dwelling on this forever. If sixty-five years aren't enough, a fair question might be, are eighty years enough?

Are a hundred years enough?

At what point do we let it go?

After having written that book, after having "discovered" all of this about life, your life, do you feel any less anxious about death and the steep angle of your own physical decline?

Another way to ask this is to say, does self-awareness mitigate fixation?

Are we out of time?

Do you have a few more minutes?

Have you ever for a single second in your entire life escaped from the carapace of yourself?

Ever really entered the world?

Not to mention embraced the world?

You absolutely love self-quarantining, don't you? I knew it.

I mean, if you had to do it all over again, what would you fundamentally alter about your angle of attack or, perhaps, angle of retreat?

Has your entire life been a bit of a nonstarter?

Your career as well?

How earnestly have you been contemplating suicide of late?

Your father tried and failed many times, so here's your chance to succeed?

We're sitting together on the fifth-floor balcony of my apartment. What's to stop us?

I mean you—what's to stop *you*?

Would that be too linear?

Too "narrative"?

Too "predictable"?

Too "commercial"?

Too cinematic?

Too melodramatic?

Too much blood and guts for your fragile sensibility?

Too active?

Too "out there"?

Too overt?

Too "real"?

Oh, that's good; the very self-consciousness that has paralyzed you your whole life will now provide a temporary reprieve for you. Had you planned that all along?

That's too perfect, is it not?

Comedy

The essence of comedy is the mechanical encrusted upon the living.

—HENRI BERGSON

WE KNOW COMEDY isn't pretty; so, too, is it ever not cruel?

I mean, are you trying to make me uncomfortable?

Do swear words possess even the slightest power anymore?

Do dirty jokes?

Would you like to tell us one?

Too namby-pamby for you?

So we're back to talking some more about you, then—how formative it was for you as a California kid to listen to four hours of slightly risqué comedy every Saturday night on KPFA when you yourself could not say a single sentence?

How do any of us—you included—escape the doldrums of reality?

Other than talking to another human being?

Are illusions better than nothing?

What else can we do?

What else are there but dreams, phantoms, other people?

I was trying to remember the last time I had laughed as hard, and I thought of Houellebecq's *Whatever*; did you ever read that?

Seriously?

Him?

Were you disappointed that some of the critics didn't pick up on the humor?

That book was all about irony, was it not?

Could you read aloud that passage I found particularly funny?

But really nothing beyond that?

A cure for irony?

It's pretty hardwired into the human condition, wouldn't you say?

That's what Wallace got wrong, in your view?

Do you—did you—find life fun?

It can't all be one long death spiral, can it?

Too bad there aren't people here; they could be asking questions right about now. What might they ask?

If every joke is an epigraph on the death of a feeling, then your lifelong obsession with stand-up makes you ... what ... kind of a serial killer of feelings, then?

Did people laugh, at least a little?

Was it kind of a joke?

Do you remember the line?

How does it go?

Really funny?

No final questions, comments, quibbles, brickbats?

And Errol would then play the piano on the tarmac? Amazing.

Was the whole suicide thread just a ruse, then?

A "joke"?

A not very funny joke?

How ironic are you being, even now?

How serious, behind this rather elaborate and somewhat tedious mask of "irony"?

Isn't that like an impotent man vowing abstinence?

Next

I have seen the future, and it doesn't work.

—ROBERT FULFORD

DO YOU THINK of this as the last book you'll ever write?

Oh—what's your next project?

Does each book light the match for the next one, then, almost like chain-smoking?

You've written books about stuttering, basketball, "morality," celebrity "culture," race, vicariousness, mistranslation, the "new autobiography," the American industrial sports complex, death and dying, "reality," loneliness, fake documents, literature, J. D. Salinger, the life-versus-art "dilemma," suicide, brevity, marriage, masculinity, sexual trauma, war photography, "other people,"

Donald Trump, and porn. What if anything connects these rather disparate topics?

When do we get to read your next novel?

Is that really fiction, though?

Could you imagine writing a straightforward novel?

How about a sequel to that growing-up novel of yours? I'd love to know what those "characters" are doing now.

Of all the books ever written, which one do you wish you had written?

Really?

All seven—or just the first?

Is it fair to say that you've entered a late or last stage of your career?

Do you have any gas left?

Can you imagine getting to a place where you don't write anymore?

Would that perhaps be a relief?

How about a place where you don't even read anymore?

Are you nearing that stage?

What book—that you've written—has changed your life the most?

What book—that you've read—has changed your life the most?

Where are you headed tonight?

Pretty much now?

May I come with? I'm very careful, as you can see, in all covid-related matters.

For all of us, the plane is going down; what are you doing to slow its descent?

What do you see around the next bend, then?

On the horizon?

When you imagine the future without yourself in it, how does that make you feel?

What is it like being old, or at least older?

Feel super-duper satisfied about the overall journey?

How do you calculate the precise balance between the force for good and the force for ill—not only within yourself but also all of humanity?

It's all very G. K. Chesterton, isn't it?

As in, "What's wrong with the world? I am."

That appeals to you, does it? Shocker.

When can we look for your next film?

Looking back upon your output, what do you see?

What are the zeniths?

The nadirs?

You keep looking at your watch. I don't know anyone who wears a watch anymore. Do you have to be somewhere soon?

How do we get through the pandemic?

And then will we survive global warming?

What are you personally doing to combat climate change?

Any thoughts on what the next big cultural wave will be?

Half of your former students work for Amazon. I'd love to see you write an up-close, very insider, gossipy, book-length eviscer-ation—any chance?

What do you definitely not want to write?

Are we done?

Are you done?

Is that what that gesture means?

DAVID SHIELDS is the author of more than twenty books, including *Reality Hunger* (recently named one of the most important books of the last decade by *Lit Hub*), *The Thing About Life Is That One Day You'll Be Dead* (a *New York Times* bestseller), *Black Planet* (a finalist for the National Book Critics Circle Award), and *Other People: Takes & Mistakes* (a *New York Times Book Review* Editors' Choice).

Nobody Hates Trump More Than Trump: An Intervention was published in 2018. *The Trouble with Men: Reflections on Sex, Love, Marriage, Porn, and Power* appeared in 2019.

James Franco's film adaptation of *I Think You're Totally Wrong: A Quarrel*, which Shields co-wrote and co-stars in, was released in 2017. Shields wrote, produced, and directed *Lynch: A History*, a 2019 documentary about Marshawn Lynch's use of silence, echo, and mimicry as key tools of resistance.

A recipient of Guggenheim and NEA fellowships, a senior contributing editor of *Conjunctions*, and the Loren Douglas Milliman Distinguished Writer-in-Residence at the University of Washington in Seattle, Shields has published fiction and nonfiction in *The New York Times Magazine*, *Harper's*, *Esquire*, *The Yale Review*, *Salon*, *Slate*, *Tin House*, *A Public Space*, *McSweeney's*, *The Believer*, *HuffPost*, *Los Angeles Review of Books*, and *Best American Essays*. His work has been translated into two dozen languages.